Robert Gibbs

DRIVING TO OUR EDGE

Many of these poems have appeared in the *New Brunswick Reader*, the *Antigonish Review*, *TickleAce*, *Gaspereau Review*, the *Cormorant*, the *Nashwaak Review*, *Poetry Canada Review* and *Pottersfield Portfolio*. "Jackie's Poems" appeared as a foreward to *Beforehand: the Poetry of Jacqueline Dyck Akkouh* and "RG" appeared in a special issue in memory of Ralph Gustafson of *Journal of Eastern Township Studies* 9.

We acknowledge the support of the Canada Council for the Arts, the Ontario Arts Council, the Government of Ontario through the Ontario Media Development Corporation's Ontario Book Initiative, the Government of Canada through the Book Publishing Industry Development Program and others for our publishing activities.

Cover art by Jennifer Garrett. Typesetting and book design by Michael Macklem

ISBN 0 7780 1226 3 (hardcover)
ISBN 0 7780 1227 1 (softcover)

ONTARIO ARTS COUNCIL
CONSEIL DES ARTS DE L'ONTARIO

Printed in Canada

PUBLISHED IN CANADA BY OBERON PRESS

For Bob and Peggy Hawkes and for Peggy's students, past and present

DRIVING TO OUR EDGE

DRIVING TO OUR EDGE

We're driving through summer haze
east to the shore through heaviness
We're driving east over back
roads patched-over patches
by woods slashed and burnt gloamed

and dripping ditches stitched along
by purple vetch pricked out
with thistles   We're driving east this
morning to the smell of it the sea
seawater and seawinds

breathing their stuff inward through fine
needles hemlocks and hackmatacks
sweetfern and sweetclover
clean breaths from out where the moon
from behind veils and veils pulls

to rake and unrake yesterday's
sand castles to comb and uncomb
dune grasses and strand vile
jellies purple opaque cyclopean
among the pea-blossoms and sand-

flies stewing   We're driving
to our edge its tongues torn
a thousand times and mended its ghosts
lost a thousand times and found
in seabirds crying shorebirds running

SUMMER ANIMATIONS

She is not more anxious than I
this large-handed mother I
a bystander to her and her kids
on the bridge two boys
both fidgety for the fireworks
to start   She clutches one by the pants
then the other a six-year-old
and a four by my guess   They clamour
and whine and climb the wide railings

Alternately they hang their heads over
to spit down at the dark river where
bats scoop and swoop after moths
She scolds and threatens and cajoles
She sighs over at me with her eyes

I know how you feel I say to myself
and think back to how they do too

Forty small boats line
the upper bridge   The river warps
their lights   For them and for her and for me
this wait's too long   I've come
down the trail to see the tail-end
of frolics the last blooms on our country's
birthday

I came alone with only Venus above
clear of murkiness a still night
heavy with vanilla and allspice from
basswood flowers and the clean acridness
of sticky poplars   Daisies
confirmed dim firmaments along the path
Fidgets of midges did their bit
to animate the air

At last the cracks and crackles
bolt upward to toss out blooms
one over another shorter
than eyewinks Teenagers
at my elbow holler out *Awesome*
and *Cool* and *Oh that's my favourite*
or *Ooh that one sucks*   A jolly volley
at which the four-year-old buries
his head in his mum's jeans
means the show is over

We back off the railings and race
to beat the mob they to their cars
me to my trail now
a ghost of itself   Lightning bugs
blink their on-off signals
both sides the path a commerce
of love and lovers to see me
home and unbedazzle my eyes

1492/1992

I

*On the first leg of the journey, Pinta's rudder jumped its
gudgeons — Samuel Eliot Morrison.*

Yes that's what rudders of small
craft do jump their gudgeons on

maybe any leg of the journey   And
as for legs a nightwatch is a

millipede or multimillipede its
pace a second-by-second creep

ticked off by heartbeats   So
my prayer must be one to

the gudgeons as pivot-pins and
my breakfast flatbread and beans and

flat water till the red line
makes the right cross on the uncharted

dark   Still there' a taste in these
mornings *el gusto de las mañanas*

II

that's more sweet than salt   It's
the taste of hacking a path through woods

without knowing what they'll
open into   It's the taste of

wintergreen's ribby round
leaves at the edge of mosses

hardly chewable but yielding cool
medicine for a stuck tongue   It's

the taste of a whitethroat's last
peabody its springsong broken the taste

of a cook's nose for a secret mushroom
of an eye's eye for a plain text

*Our great globe floated in the atmosphere of infinite space
like an insubstantial bubble — Nathaniel Hawthorne.*

I saw a light like a little wax candle
rising and falling   I heard a wind sift
through pine needles like a fine rain
Then my spirit left my body as a moth

leaves its broken house in the dark and goes
spellbound toward a lantern hung from a mast
a spirit out of the night flying to where
the bent world turns round below it

I saw the green of a green place sicken and
pale past yellow into grey   The sun's
red eye opening over the edge
singed trees of weeping habit and

scorched lizards belly-up   Cries
caked together from nests and nestlings
flamed and shrivelled   I saw boulders
grind their teeth and all the icecaps

weep   I was there at the ends of the world
Then I heard someone shout *Tierra tierra*
and I knew that the globe of my body was there
where I left it and my voyagings not done

AGB

From one of his students

Eyes that scanned the light
along horizons and over
them turned inward

on their outward watch
Hands on a wheel that kept
us pointed while not

appearing to through under-
tows and tidestrifes and
shoaled eddies to a sweet

and reasonable harbour
I never quite learned
to call you Alfie for years

Dr. Bailey as due
though not demanded then
AGB as

how you announced yourself
It's still your voice
that quiets my disquiet a voice

that listened while it spoke
as attentive to us as to
its own imperatives connectives

14

and disconnectives poetry's
logic through all your disciplines
You left and still leave

in ears and hearts that listen
word of your travels and light too
a horizon just now crossed

15

BLUE MOON BLUES

A moon second-to-the-last
in this millennium looms
blue out of the east in daylight
thin as onionskin but still
overbearing a growing ghost

One of these last-of-January days
in this penultimate year
it will shine all night and turn
down here into its own kind
of mindscape snow piled around
everywhere pitted and shrunk by thaws
and specked with unspeculative dust

I'll rise at four in the morning to hike
the thermostat and look out
at the floodlit yard rigid
and glossy I'll hear winded
chimes peal an unappealing jangle
rocked faintly in their own imbalances

the very air fixed in dogma
code of a pitted face an unpitying
eye

Then the ribs old ribs of an old
house will crack with a gunshot report
to end the on-dreaming of dreams
and start the on-whispering of names
names I know and names I don't
my breath a smoke pillow still
a snowhill my animus
anonymous anomalous

But somewhere out there
(up there in here) father
still my father catch my breath

ELEGIES FOR MAISIE

1978-1998

I

A week ago on a snowy Tuesday
I took Maisie to the vet and didn't
bring her back   Almost twenty
years ago I picked her out
from a ball of siblings all
scarcely weaned   I named her
for the fierce M above her mild
eyes though it might have been
for the maze of tabby markings
butterflies and all decoded
from her genesis the first feline

brought to Adam with *Now here's*
something different to which
he might have said *Now*
I'd call that a cool cat

2

Maisie you in all your ways
were a most cat-like cat
Your blunt front would register
disdain more often than disgust
indignation more than rage
content more than delight
The motor in your throat never
gave out even when your legs
did   It trilled on
an underground stream
subversive to grids and chokers

3

And what did Maisie like most?
Her Saturday-breakfast kipper or
lying perfectly hid with sun
and shadow dappling her black
and tarnished silver her mellow
gold under the blooming currant
bush in wait for birds hummingbirds
she'd bat down to play with
(I rescued more than one of them) or
resting at her last post beside
the wicker elephant at the foot
of the stairs (with the world on its back)
where she would greet each passerby
in the night and cheer breakfast on

These she may have dreamed on
in her much-dreaming days
These she may dream on now
in her much deeper sleep

NOT FOR GROUNDLINGS

We sit lightly icecream
cones in hand and glide up
the Thames Greenwich to Westminster
Past the blocked docklands and
Canary Wharf with its ramps and
struts and town-topping pyramid
that gleams the cold gleam
of pounds sterling we swivel
in our seats boxed-in pews
of our wooden sanctuary and
tune out of our ears
our guide's canned cockney

I keep saying to my sister
*Watch out for the Globe   It should be
coming up left round
the next bend*   Sure enough

there it is thatched as cosily
into its niche between walls of windows
as if it were not the mere ghost
of Hamlet's ghost and all those other
apparitions hatched in the lobes
of Will Shakespeare's own
globe his unmatched hemispheres

Father Thames snakes round to
circumvent conclusions as one
arena circles another and one
race encompasses them all
run or crawled or ridden
over this midden we call home

Gentrified warehouses with one balcony
topping another for proliferating
balcony scenes up to those with top
tickets   Not for groundlings
I think   Nobody I know gets
to sit where they sit

Still from another view
the more saintly saints must be
overlooking it all from their
winner's circle next to
the royal enclosure

To them we're all
groundlings gawkers and squawkers
brawlers who've paid their coppers
for a last ferryride upriver
past the past recast groundlings
dirt of the dirt we dig in

yet loved
with an unreasonable love
like the one Will Shakespeare
must have had for all
his scrappy rabbles up and on
his old Globe's apron or
in its pit down below

A POST-CHRISTMAS CAROL

In the bleak midwinter choirboys sing
voices as untainted as snowflakes on a swing

I like to think of shelter for all that friendly crew
and the child as lowly ox and ass and ewe

dumb before the shearer tough to whip and goad
born to do the carrying not to be the load

Even snooty camels have to learn to kneel
before high-crowned magi can try out their skill

News comes on of horses that stumble out-of-doors
eleven down-country leavings from old wars

Their shelter makeshift ribbed like their sides
nose to nose they nicker lice in their hides

their dead half-buried or dragged to the woods
breakfast for foxes supper for their broods

Why all this outcry? someone justly frowns
Children go as hungry right in our towns

earth stood hard as iron chills more than cheers
no quick fixes and no going shares

A stall and some fodder a pat on the nose
all a beast asks for to make it nuzzle close

The beadle's friendly wisemen designate shelves
where kids without voices will live inside themselves

Why all the outcry? Because they are dumb
They'll freeze uncomplaining till someone finds them room

Snow has fallen snow on snow   Will coldness never end?
and Guernica's broken critters find a way to mend?

24

FOREBEARS & FORBEARANCES

I

A long way north and west from
the English fens with their square towers
and Ely's ghost cathedral looming
out of mists past Bedford
and Bunyan's gaol into high
country hedges giving way to
stone walls and rounded hills
pocked with rabbit holes   I'd left
my bike in a layby and climbed a stile

Who knows how long I'd been pumping
on my old three-speed bought
from the college bikeman for twelve-and-six
Now night was coming and my bones
knew it and turned my head inward

2

It was late October and the bracken
on the moor-like rises a dark earth
colour   the fields pale stubble   and
the low places flagged and plumed
with cattails   It was rough country
but open   big-sky   like I
was later to find in dry-grass
prairie   a sky to inhale and halloo in

I'd found a matted track and followed
it down to where the sun sank and
up to where it rose again
just above the bracken   Then I saw
the house   crouched and spread like a
ground-nesting bird or a sprawled
outcropping from the earth itself

A light that flickered and steadied drew
my eyes to it   At least there'll be
a barn or haystack where I
can burrow in for the night

26

3

I remembered that night at the head
of Dovedale when Louis and I
took shelter in a farmhouse and the
farm daughter showed us how
to bottle-feed two orphan lambs

We'd reached the village and its one pub
on foot ravenous our sausage-rolls
long since consumed only
to find they served not even
a pretzel   So we filled up on stout
as black and solid as blackstrap
molasses and at their direction tottered
up to the farm singing our silly
lungs out   Maybe there
in that spread of low eaves
I'll get a similar welcome and a bed
with breakfast for a few bob

4

I held to the track for surely
though it dipped and meandered through
swamps and around hillocks its direction
was steady toward that steadying light

5

Who knows how long it took
but the day held and the first star
came out a second beacon above
the other on the red-eyed gloaming

6

This is what comes of searching out
ancestral sites forebears and forbearances
How many days was I at it?   And
from this distance how much
is memory how much dream?

7

Down into such a pitch dark
I could feel breaths breathing
on my nape the unseen apollyan
of my earliest dreams I could hear
the thud of my own heart echoed
in footsteps behind My own
foot slipped into some kind of muck
or deep-sucking quicksand
I pulled it free and the matted track
turned upward back into the halflight

8

Here it was in front of me
no farmhouse but an inn spreading
its coverts thatched and half-timbered
tudor at least with leaded bays
and oriels some catching the last
glints and some lit from inside

I lifted the knocker and let it fall
on what I knew was my own door

A host as rounded as a host should be
showed me in and up a stairway
Expecting me all along he said

9

When I awoke the second time
(the first was an inside event)
I knew the place I'd been ample
and furnished amply too in dark
woods and leathers wainscotted
where it wasn't walled with books
its outlook ample and its hearth

Downstairs in the kitchen I knew
I'd find him the king rocking
in his carpet-backed rocker beside
the great iron-and-nickel stove
where the queen stood turning
breakfast sausages in a pan

She'd smile me to my place among
her sons and daughters muffins
and honey and breakfast laughter

10

When I awoke the third time
I knew I'd be pumping back
over and over that road looking for
my layby my stile my matted track

30

LIKE YOU AND LIKE I

I wonder as I wander out under the sky
how Jesus the saviour came down for to die
for poor ornery sinners like you and like I
I wonder as I wander out under the sky

I

A thief comes out of lifting fog
I watch from a side window and sip my second
after-breakfast tea. She sits high
and rides one-handed a black plastic
bag slung over her left shoulder

She drops her bike to the curb and swings
her bag over her head and down   She'll add it
to the pile my neighbour's garbage   But no
she's opened its throat and with two sweeps
of her hand has scoffed in all the cans and
bottles from the blue box of my goodwill
neighbours   I'm up and out of there ready

to stand on guard O Canada for our week's
offering one tomato-juice can   She's seen
me though she hasn't looked my way
Head high and eyes front she's lost
none of her dignity   I see her close up
and my politically-correct wrath drains

She rides on her face not old
but marked with hard markings unmade-up
a face used perhaps abused but strong
her brown hair caught back   Neat and clean

she's doing what she's doing cycling
and recycling for dimes and nickels not
because she enjoys scrobbling from innocent
blue baskets but because she's driven
and held to it by something or someone
hard and immovable as rock
or the resigned reserve of her own face

32

The first time I passed its false-brick front
and plain slogan *North Side Redemption
Centre* I thought it was a church
modest yet assertive like other small ones
around here with names like *Ark of Safety
Family Refuge* or *Cleft-in-the-Rock
Community Chapel* (not those but names
like those) soul-saving and foot-washing
stations for weary pilgrims Then I saw
a van back in and unload a week's empties
cases and cases testimony to hard
parties and maybe harder partings

Whether at an altar-rail or confessor's box
or sad old mourner's bench it's good
to have a place to unload your load
to redeem whatever's redeemable refill
whatever's refillable and recycle
(you know the rest) Monday's
our garbage day and good-citizen blue-box
day Sometimes it takes a scavenger or two
to scour the road ahead through dark woods

"OUR BONES ARE SCATTERED
AT THE GRAVE'S MOUTH"

I

The wild apple tree behind our house
has blossomed out and atomized
the air with its strong sweetness

Last Sunday they buried the bones
of an unknown soldier one of 20,000
in Ottawa with great ceremony

A week earlier in France
they buried bones and dogtags
found in a field by a tourist
another Canadian put to rest
with great ceremony   Veterans
at both wiped tears from their eyes
their innocence reclaimed in solemn rites

And what about your bones James?
The century rolled up behind me
leaves much I can't scrape
off my heels like the calluses
that have hardened over winter

2

Trees keep close daybooks
closer than mine and in them
balance windblasts and whispers
sun and sweet rain   To make peace
with my days I root among
records for any account of you
James whose violent death fourteen
years ago has only this spring
come to my notice   I'm not good
at balancing books but must try
at least for the record's sake

35

3

A special-needs kid they'd call
you now But looking back at others
held in my scanty archive I'd call
you all that my Grade-9 pupils
of 40 years ago

A gawky teenager pale-faced
wry-necked and dark-eyed
eyes that smouldered or brightened
with wild laughter or rage

I remember how you loped
down school hallways and shouted
I'm a lunatic   I'm a lunatic
and the other kids said *That James
he's crazy isn't he sir*

This tree will set fruit gnarled
and scabby no doubt but sweet
and full of seeds some of which
will find ground to rest in

36

4

What I remember most about you
James (never Jim or Jimmy)
were the stories you wrote
for composition class man-and-boy
stories you and your absentee dad
in wild adventures dogfights
in a plane he taught you to fly

They found you James
in a parking-lot between two churches
Calvary and Trinity   The rector of the latter
said you were seeking sanctuary
(but you'd been stabbed to death)

Can I by the ceremony
of making verses give rest
to what I can't add up?
You a troubled kid but no more
crazy than the others clean
and well groomed plainly
looked after in some sense

I don't think I can except
to assert an innocence reclaimed
as in the eyes of those old soldiers

HALE-BOPP SYNDROME

HALE-BOPP SYNDROME

This little river has carved
a canyon for itself to snake through
down to an outlet under the fence

where it cascades into snow-sponge
Generations of frost laid down
through storms and thaws of this

latest ice age hold unnibbled
by the sun that plays peekaboo
with the northwest corner   It will take

a lot of weeping to make a heartbeat
quiver in this stone   It will take
more than one penitential

psalm streaming back from the comet
overhead to free these doors to shut
and open   Finches twitterfill the air

and chickadees practise lovenotes
one falling off another
sadly   I must exit gingerly

at first light tomorrow   I must
forestall garbled bassoons goosenotes
with my own broken calls

ALDEN-AND-ROBBIE'S DAY

25 January

When winter stays in place cold and white
under pine-needles under snow
the shrew lives out her January   Doves
scatter and tail-over-head squirrels
skitter blue on the perfect yard   Shrew
noses out of her tunnel gingerly as an angel
to lip a sunflower seed and slip back

Maybe she has babies in there to pull
on her nailpoint nipples   How much
deeper in her bunker she has to hunker
in these days of January thaw before
the wind turns back to his proper quarter
and snuffs improper green with whitestuff
Today in particular meeting-place

of two poets' birthdays so wide
apart yet nearer to each other each
time they happen Alden-and-Robbie's day
Peculiar it should be so dark this noon
crepuscular a half-poet might call it a
louring glowering sky yet not un-
befitting two born to lopsided days

and nights two who warmed themselves
and us with hot brews and distillates who
died both early withdrawn from us yet
as much here as the shrew's nose
that pokes out quivering over and over
questing questioning whatever light there is
to take from it her winter bread

BROWN-EYED ANGELS

Flights out of summer
to cricket wheedles and
scissor-sharpeners along
the path and birds'urgings
subsume what's here and gone
to what's ahead

And for speedups
wheel-shaped asters
circle fenceposts and caution
day-lilies in tattered gardens
to number their days

Tiny white stars
asterisk byways as if to signal
Look to the endnotes you
stragglers and strugglers

Aster colours pale blues
and lavenders foreshadow
snow shadows

Frosty galaxies drift
across seasons to butt
edgy ghosts smokes that last
low suns will exhale
and smudge demarcations

43

Scythes sharpen and cutlasses
to cut loose fettered grasses

Brown-eyed angels
muster on borderlands
whose oats run wild and overripe

AN OCTOBER RAMBLE
THROUGH PAIN

I

There's litle flesh between them
the dancing-master and his johnny   On these
cold fall days at the market's
north gate their lips and fingers are
alike blue   Whoever made this mannekin
fashioned him to jiggle not to jig
to fortyish tunes from a fortyish radio

My grandfather Charles Wortman Tower
and his cousin Nathan Hoar noted
for their featly-jointed dancing-jacks
all over their county could go
like everything my mother said
They fingered every figure as flawlessly
as their own feet could foot them they
of the O'Brien clan famous for nimbleness
in limb and tongue   And great-grandmother
Orenda O'Brien Tower if a fiddler
were kept from his fiddle would mouth the tunes
as aptly and stitch into them her calls
and cautions seamlessly for the dancers to dance to

Fiddle diddle dum dee I don't know
Fiddle diddle dum dee   Maybe so
You take that thing to be your beau
I tell you lass where you can go

3

Curbed by a MacQuarrie's literal
sagacity tempered by a Hoar's disdain
for natural work by their gift of gab
my centre of gravity sacked too low
to give my feet dancing room
I was one for whom my sister chose
as family motto   *There's a divinity*
that shapes our ends rough hew
them how we will and so I turned to words

4

At my age beginning to see
this ossuary's softer than the bones
it houses spongy knees over-leavened
loaves   I hear from inside a jangle
of coathangers loosely belted together
at the collar and at the girdle from which
appendages no more apt than that market
dancing-man's drip and dangle
And the seat of my pain is not
where the doctors say it is but in that grave
centre toward which my declivities flow

5

You friend stood by the night
this pain started not to smile on me
with special promises of relief but
to light my head with oil and have
me remember Job and how he was
sifted and Nebuchadnezzar when
I found myself lying under
my footstool a most biblical position
you'll agree   Moving out from there
first on my belly then four-footed
reeling from that far-off
recapitulation   I skipped the riddle
and with my sturdy third rose
to full height a man rethroned

6

I leave bipedalism to the penguins
They do it best even better than
those diminutive golfers with
perpetually elevated bills who strut
their fairways to catch their ball's
fall from heaven onto the next green

A POOR-SUCKER SAMARITAN
SAYS ENOUGH ALREADY

You Sir Acrobat I've had
just about enough of   And that
goes for all your troupe antics
out of keeping with the season and mean
ones at that   There you are
stuck all down the feeder
like a slug extended to cover every
access your busy little thief's
hands can paw the stuff out of
black-oil seeds the size and colour
of your own popped-out eyes

And that Sir is the third feeder
we've put out this year
the other two one an Audubon
certified and sanctified
by its name the second glassy
as the bottle it was modelled on
chewed through in two days

The chickadees share my grief
when my brother calls from the kitchen
They've got it down again
While the doves huddle and mutter
in the bare-bones birchtree
ready to descend on the spillage

None of my baffles have baffled you
tinfoil pie-plates
no foil to the dig-ins of your pink
naked toenails   Sir even the skunks
had the grace to retire from raids
on our compost box once they'd managed
to tumble off the lid and shatter it
They show respect to the season
of peace and goodwill and withdrawal
from acts of vandalism against
our poor plastic contrivances

And we retire too into deep
easychairs and long old books
our heads can nod over
and nobody know the difference except
perhaps the Lord who hears and heeds
the chickadees scolding and makes
us hear them too once you've wrestled
(not content with what your paws
can paw out of the proper holes)
our newest plastic feeder to the ground

and slid it in shame down the bank
to the bottom and rolled it
and frisked it and left it so to say
bruised and broken on the Jericho road
for a poor-sucker Samaritan like me

to go out into blood-freezing
semi-darkness in my slippers to mute
the calls that call from branches overhead

NEW YEAR'S SHUFFLE

I'll walk out again before
the snow flies   just as
the old year's giving place

the time and tune my feet sing by
still *Jesus Loves Me* as they
crunch frozen gravel notched
to a higher-than-summer pitch

Milkweed ears unflossed
rattle with every riffle
but lime-green mullein younglings
put to shame my own
bloodless appendages

Dogwood osiers burn crimson
against a greyed-out scheme
and redpolls skite beside me
end-over-end   clump to clump
and rose-hip to rose-hip   cheerily

Pigeons ranged southward
on the old log-balk beside the bridge
will puff out to catch whatever
sun the day's low circuit can muster
and shimmer in it

I'll mark again the dome
glimmer white through birches
a mini-taj whose postulants
range along the river bank
site of old Fort Nashwaak
memory of a memory ghost of ghosts

All the way over my belly
warmed at Tim Horton's I'll turn
north again and let the mendicant
sun place a hand on my back
and call old aches to heel

EASTER WEEKEND '93

I

A sky eggshell blue for a
perfect holy day and grey
feathers shed at shoulders
for yellowing finches   Bloom-hazes
purple and magenta cancel
uprights and their arms

Across my shoulders a bass arioso
from the *St. Matthew Passion* reconfirms
with Bach and Bible cartilage
darker co-ordinates

2

We drive north on Good Friday
the river on our left open
with white wafers on it as far
as the dam then closed with
turtleback medallions breaking
all the way up to the headpond

Fields pied with snow match
Holstein huddles that stick close
to barnyards   Sumac candelabras
flaunt gobbets of last year's
blood   Birches and dogwoods
tingle with sap to their tips
and every maple sports its sapcan
badge   Trucks trundle vats
and barrels of April sweetstuff

3

We will cross at Woodstock and stop
to walk a circuit along to a graveyard
where our great grandmother may be
waiting then back along the river
to where the Meduxnekeag thrusts in
to start breakup its cakes caking
high on both banks   We'll hold
the river to our left driving home
and wonder if the Indians at Kingsclear
have lifted their barricade and whether
the standoff with the mounties has led
to shots or truncheons and how many
beside the chief have been carted off

4

We come to the remnants a dark
mound of them with fires smouldering
well off the road well flanked with flashing
reds and blues   A blueblack bus spills
men in blueblack gear and we think
of yesterday when we ran
smack into St Mary's band's blockade
of Dedham Street with its sad banners
that told us of something we still hadn't
got from them   The one-armed
drumming dims behind us and the rise
and fall of voices lamenting earth's
lament and sky's

5

White fanfares for Easter Day flank
the altar broken wafers and drumnotes
announcements and benedictions   Outside
dark rains soften riverthroats

CHORAL SEASON

For Sister Lorette Gallant

Choir-time bird-and-kid
music-festival time and here
on the undersea floor
of the hemlock woods it's
dogtooth-violet time sifted light
and sifted sage and crusted hulks
where we walk ears cocked
to the singing of singing birds

Dad you were a Trinity
choir-boy white-surpliced
and all   And you kept a true
bassline once your voice dropped
from treble   And I too

in Grade 6 was a kind of
choir-boy one of a strand
of boys cowed into doing
The Ash Grove
in the local festival   Shakily
I held on to the descant carried aloft
by Ted a Trinity-trained soprano

We didn't come in first or
even second as I recall though
George our conductor ogred us
into expressiveness with every possible
stretch of his rubber face

A week ago I sat on stage
kitty-cornered to the risers where
Les Jeunes Chanteurs would rise
and soar in French and English
every i dotted and every
t crossed in perfect pitch
and diction their tones
pure as these bells that brighten
the sunshine that threads through needles
onto this beech-leaf seafloor

And there was the sister
Sister Lorette unchanged
from when I first saw her
more than twenty years ago

her choir too the same blend
of voices the same unending phrases
relayed as seamlessly as the threads
of their counterpoint stitched in

Sitting as I was half
facing her and half them
I could see how much they
were hers and she theirs
Eyes gave and received a like
brightness as her hands and arms
shaped the air between them
into their airs their answers

3

Great ensembles down the decades
don't lose resemblance whoever
the personnel lost or gained
One pair of ears has formed
them informed them reformed

George our choirmaster was at pains
visible agonies even just
to keep our tones from wandering
like our song's streamlets off
the tune into some yonder valley

4

A chickadee chooses this moment
to call his two-note pure
spring call his raspier song
tucked well back in his throat
for a less choral season

MORNING BELLS AND WARNING BELLS

Man's life's a vapour full of woes
That's part of an old rhyme sung
as a round and only partly true

Rounds are fun   I like their possibility
of going on and on   They circle
and come back to you like days
and daylight even pale daylight

A round is not a relay but like one
except that as you hand back the baton
you reach ahead to catch the one
tossed back to you   That's why
they used to call them catches

Once you're in a round you're more
or less obliged to keep your part going
for as long as anyone else has breath
Then one by one singers drop off
and the round stops

He cuts a caper and down he goes
True enough but sometimes it should say
up he goes   Seasons are like that
rondos capricioso always recurring
sometimes with mellow cellos and sometimes
with abrupt gongs that shiver
and make you quiver

59

November comes like that bleached
and leeched but with blood-coloured
poppies and the same old songs
Pack up your troubles in your old kit bag
and *Keep the home fires burning*   They
warm and chill you at the same time

Miss Carvell my Grade 3 teacher
wielded her pointer like a conductor's baton
when she clicked up and down the rows
and taught us my first round *Oh how lovely*
is the evening is the evening

Like other rounds it ends in bells
Ding dong Ding dong Ding dong
Once they've entered they set a drone
or a bass   Boys like to boom them out
and test their manhood on them

I like especially the French round
Le bourdon dit à la clochette
where big-brother bell scolds
the little-brother one who insists on his
din-dong din-dong din-dong din-dong
though he knows he'll never catch up

As for the man who cuts a caper
Down and down and down and down
and down he goes   Let him
be a lesson to us all!

LOONYSSEY

We ride our dad's back
a good place to be only
crowded with my brother's big
feet He's up there
asleep his head drooped
over on our dad's white
shirtfront He's smoky and fuzzy
like me I guess But our dad's
slick as a whistle and he carries
whole skies on his sides

You can see them all spangly
with stars that glimmer back
from below I ride like Dad
with my eyes open His dark
gold ones never shut
His spear's pointed straight
ahead to where we're going
(We don't have to know
my brother and I as long
as we're with him) He holds

himself half under
His big paddles beat
slow and steady way
in there   But you should see
him dive and swim down there
faster than he does up here
(though not when we're riding
on him)   And he
can pick out silver fish streaks
and go after them till he

spears them then come back
to where he's left us
on some grassy bit
of island and feed them
to us   When dark comes
he calls his long calls
They shake the twilight like
those shimmers out of the north
that colour the sky crazy
then go out faster

than they came   They make
your bones shiver   We're
learning to swim and already
we paddle around a little
Some day we'll fly
not too well but maybe
as well as our dad does
and that's well enough
Meantime
we'll ride

63

THE IRISHNESS OF SUMMER

The green sides of daylight are sides
of a stone an emerald May's stone
or Mary's kept into summer hard

burning summer   Seven shades
of green a prism's worth my eye
looks into as into a leaded

window and down into a crypt
lit with apocalyptic lights that will
call worms out of holes

chicks out of nests songs
out of throats branded and
choked but freed let loose by the

Irishness of summer its wolfhound
keenings and holy mawkishness
Under all this green

red bedded in waits
its turn to answer the way an organ
answers calls to prayer by gorging

on the air pumped into it   Red
will masticate all this in its time
the woods bonedry as they are but green

will keep its own three-leafed
evangel against the kicks and pricks
of wasps and leggy hoppers

"DEATH MIGHT MEAN
THE EMPTIED VOICE"

The moon in her last quarter gauzes over
and the falling wind disperses windchimes
The yard shines hard fields and river too
with a ghost shine   All outdoors

starts all over again with snow
sure to purify and recover everything
Yesterday I dusted my shelves   With the long
wand of my vacuum-cleaner I reached up

and groomed all fourteen stables
that house the homegrown poets from Lloyd Abbey's
"Pegasus" *plumed in morn, the unspoiled sky*
to Jan Zwicky's *Wittgenstein Elegies*

In the middle of it all dust begins to fly
like snow grey flakes of it   It swirled
round my face and settled back on the verses
I had sucked it from   My machine

gone into reverse spewed its clingy
things up my nostrils and up the poets'
spines   And I remembered John Zanes
asking Dorothy Livesay about some ashes

65

about to be buried on Forest Hill the poet's
corner in October   *And where have these ashes
been since February?   Just around gathering
dust so to speak?*   And I remembered

Dorothy just back from Zambia yellow
Kalihari dust in her lungs and throat
with her new book *The Colour of God's Face*
that begins *Implacable woman*

The turgid dustbag replaced and grooming
resumed   I nosed my dustsniffer in between
Acorn and Avison Bartlett and Brewster
Cogswell Gustafson and Klein Nowlan and

Reaney Richards Sherman and Trainer all
the way over and down to John Zanes and Jan
with her closing words *Death might mean
the emptied voice / at last begin to speak*

DEFINING NETWORKS

DEFINING NETWORKS

The woodpecker swings low
and upside-down negotiates
the branch under which the shrunken
red-orange net-ball
of suet toppled from its jute-twined
cradle swings temptingly emptied

This downy bird as sharp-eyed
as any stretches up his neck
and pecks at what mouldy crumbles
remain from the starlings' mass
scrambles   He's as sharp-dressed
as any with his red barrettes
this natty bird but seems obsessed
with extricating that last white worm
extruded from the onion-bag intact

Stretching up or out or down
wrenches links I never knew
I had he might say but he's
not into tongue-twister
chortles or rusty-hinge bill
blues   He raps out morse
rata-tat-tats to hollow
out a space in the crowded spring
network for his own kin and kind

In the soft creases where lights
go off and on the woodpecker
knows as any lexicographer
even Sam Johnson knows
what is reticulated and decussated
and what is not the hole and the worm
in the hole a gift without repentance

69

RG

For Betty Gustafson in memory of Ralph

Look, you have had love and though
Now alone, the birds are swift
In the grain where ripe fruit is
— Early Summer.

1

The initials are the same
his and mine but not
ear or eye or heart
I can make no claim

I'd have to wear a jeweller's
eyeglass screwed in
to fix as he fixed
onto and into crocuses
through cracks in tiles
mosaics Greek and Venetian
on his globewide glebe
fixed them in his viking scop's
scope true and blue

And what an earpiece I'd
have to affix or implant
to finger his figures
his gigues across fissures
pointed and counterpointed

And when I read the poems
I can hear him still
startled and wary bemused
and rueful tongue on tiptoe
to come fresh upon
trilliums in Maytime

2

We walked he and you
and I me teasing him
about his scrutineering and
poems already com-
positioning themselves in his head
words jostling and jockeying
for their say

We walked from the tourist-trekked
rectory with its low-beamed
chambers and its rook-black
cabinet whose twelve-apostled
panels Charlotte wrote about

We walked up to the moor
above the slates me
teasing him out of
exhilaration at being there
at that height and outlook
in wuthered-over heather
October-coloured with
him and you and so much love

INESCAPABLE SHACKLES

I do not place the highest value on the state,
but rather on man and humanity . . . . I cherish a
certain hope in me, a hope as a state of the
spirit — Vaclav Hamel, Time.

A man's face is creased with
twelve creases hatched
across & across with ringed

sockets & lids at half-
mast his eyes turned
sideways away from & towards

what they can & cannot
evade hazy with too much
seeing the nose stubborn

a prow tilted upward
as if to sniff the winds though
the whole cast is inward &

downward. A mole south-
east of his lower lip may
chart a way forward through

withdrawal a way of rocks
falling or about to fall
a way into & out of

K's castle   I hold
this face as dear as any
man's or woman's

battered from behind as shattered
as Beirut or Sarajevo
a face burned in '69 when

Jan Palach set
himself on fire a face
behind bars the eyes

fettered with love & hope
inescapable shackles for
a face a man a globe

WHEN MY MOTHER PLAYED
AND SANG SPIRITUAL SONGS

73

What crossed her face as she sat rocking singing
were not shadows but lights lights of the breath

under her skin in the fine capillaries flames
lights in her songs that kept her shut lids

alive wings coverings   Then that mouthmusic
that stretched her lips this way and that as she

stretched her accordion round to the old ones
she loved   They popped from eyes to fingers

in a rough hurdygurdy fashioning   Or
her hands on our old square-grand pounded

like a marimbist's mallets a dancing tympany
all the way down to the first A

and back forging off all the keys
bronzed flights of hallelujahs

74

UNCOUNTABLE THREADWAYS

The blots looked like the tails of small comets,
and the notes like large black stars.

He left his *Requiem* restless
a score to be settled   Its brightness
startles December nights
This prize book   *A Boy Musician*
was yours Dad for standing
2nd in the 4th class in 1891
when you were almost 10 at the
Central Madras School that's
still solidly there on Duke Street
I grew up with your book its gold
and blue cover embossed

with a songbird   Inside it
little Wolfgang romped with Andrew
his playmate while Nannerl
his sister scolded and the anonymous
author moralized   I tromped
up and down my scales and
heard myself hear *Evviva*
il maestro! Evviva
il cavaliere filharmonico!
And you Dad when you came
to your cello fed the same

Victorian birds and flowers
and high calls to genius
did you dream dreams?
Knowing the you I know
I'd say not   But maybe
there's more of you in me
than I imagine   Maybe standing
2nd made you hungry too
It's December 3rd little
Wolfgang's deathday
his 200th and still his notes

spark and dart and fall
sadly away while my unvoiced
songs pry at a lid
In uncountable threadways
blood keeps a hum
humming   It's snowing now
a fine steady snow   It will
muffle posthorns and wipe out
staves   It's getting
us ready you Dad and I? for a
long white glissando

JACKIE'S POEMS

A light daisylight laughter
has gone out with your smile
from Mayfield your house
in Bucks Horn Oak so English
a house in so English a village
you a Canadian prairie girl

Jean called it your famous smile
She said you flashed it Saturday
her last visit when they told you
she had come you weightless
and voiceless like Gingy your cat
in his last past-twentieth year
Your smile Jean said lit up
the room as it did your face
your last Saturday there with Mehdi
and your boys Timmy and Carl

Something brave in it always
that smile that tipped your head
and thrust out your chin to face
whatever it had to for instance
that day in May a year ago
when we visited you in hospital
after the cutting out of all
the cancer (so the doctors thought)
that had grabbed you by the gullet
You said little   You never said
much Your voice a sunbeam
played on water kept its secrets

77

In those weeks of last summer
and early autumn while you rallied
and fell back from chemical onslaughts
the poems spated urgent as if
kept in check too long

poems about pain *pain*
untalked you call it
poems of forbearance and forgiveness
words bitter and sweet you left
us with the unspoken you
we'd seen as in sunlight
fathomed under brightness

Nine poems   Nine petals
dropped from the day's eye

78

FINDERS KEEPERS

For M'Pompman's 71st

I

A certain man had new glasses
dear ones to unblear and unblur
all he needed to keep clear
gold-rimmed specs his wife
was proud to see him wear

she who moved and kept him
moving she who pushed him
out to the very end of the boardwalk
that sails above the Bouctouche dunes
then challenged him to walk back

But he lost his sharp new specs
nobody knows where just shy
of his wife's birthday with his own
celebrations soon to follow

A certain man had a car and in
that car slept a chair that
let out would roll him
overhead of dunes and dangers
when he didn't feel like walking

His car like any car
had a key a big green-handled
one to open doors and ignite
ignitions also to unlock
the trunk with its fold-in chair

On his wife's birthday readied
for a round-the-town excursion
the key lay beside her breakfast-plate
then quite simply disappeared

After a topsy-turvy ransack
of the house where they were visiting
she got on the phone to MAA
and a locksmith while he grinned
up his innocent sleeve

3

A certain man on a journey
home from a far-off place
where he'd helped to keep
his wife's birthday (his own
soon to follow) had a zip-up

ditty bag where he kept his brushes
tooth and hair and toothpaste
and all his medications pills
to keep his head limber and his arms
and legs from jamming up

They drove from a late-April bluster
into an eastcoast fury   They got there
sound enough but found great
roots from a winded tree looming

over their driveway and the lights
all out   And the ditty bag?
Gone tossed out from the back seat
and tumbled into the woods when
they stopped to don their jackets

4

There was joy here and all over
heaven when the green-handled
key that let out the chair that
rolled him all over town
came to light in an apron pocket
that smock he'd worn at breakfast
hung on the kitchen doorknob
while his wife talked to the locksmith
the key that had grasshoppered
from beside her plate on her birthday

5

There was joy here and all over
heaven when the ditty bag appeared
unpicked and unpickled behind the salt
in the spice cupboard wafted there
by who knows whose seraphic smile

6

There was joy all around Shediac
enough for ten birthdays
when that not uncertain man came
unblundering out of his bathroom
and laughed through his gold rims

CAUSTIC ICING

VE Day fifty years after

The sun reaches around and into
a doorjamb where a spider has hung
her purse under a rusty hinge
Soon it will set afloat hundreds
of baby spiders riding their own
silks   The sun touches my father's
forehead bent to his work my mother's
hands in and out of soapsuds

Dad was an orthodox
engraver   He knew all the
alphabets italic
gothic roman block and
script   And he could make
monograms by twining M's
in and out of W's
R's in and out of G's

Mum left her pinches
on piecrust edges frail
as the meringue she topped them with
Her prints melted into
her biscuits light as the cream
she topped them with

Dandelions along the back wall
are already out bright as brass
ready to let stream an assault
of paratroopers to occupy any
free ground and dig in

Dad oiled his whetstone
his hands steadier than
his heart after it stopped
Sometimes though he'd slip
on a surface not made
for his graver a wartime
steelbacked watch or
something made of warplane-window
lucite an ID bracelet or twin hearts
for a sweetheart's brooch

Finches sing and redwings drill
and redbuds loosen with the songs
of fifty years ago *When the lights*
go on again all over the world
and *Wish me luck as you wave*
me goodbye

Mum kneels at a kitchen chair
and prays for victory
on land at sea and in the air
this day her birthday
tomorrow VE Day

A black butterfly yellow-edged
lights on the picnic table Maisie
sniffs her way down the fence
unsure of her territorial rights
now that three she-cats
a decade younger than her
have moved in next door

Dad loved the aleph beth
gimel acrostics he breakfasted
on long before any of the house
were up but him   The nicks
he made on steel or lucite
he turned into flowers
tiny sprays he filled with gold
then called us in to see taking
no credit for what he saw
as accidents accentuated

I've started turning over ground
Don with his hoe follows
to bust the clods   Frost crystals
hold on deep where worms
sleep out their sleeps in air-raid
shelters   It's time for liming
a dusting of caustic icing
sweet to acid earth

A REQUIEM FOR JIM

Who surprised us all by turning into Fr. Horner

We drove down yesterday
the back way to see you off
brought home in a box so small
your grandson Renato
only two helped his father Guillermo
carry it to the altar   And now
I'm reading your poems the only
ones I know out of old
Fiddleheads from 1952

I'm reading about *the violins*
of autumn (taken from Verlaine) and
thinking yesterday was near
fall enough for your *chromatics*
to *streak* through Charlotte County
maples   Writing then about
richly silent death you've set
me chattering and I can almost hear
your throaty chuckles loosed at any

moment appropriate or not
and your singing raspy as Miliza's
the soprano you championed over
everyone else's objections (including
those who banged on our ceiling
whenever you played her at full throat
Buck still winces at the thought
unwavering in his loyalty to Bing
more than fifty years)   I see

you as you first appeared blond
as an angel ensconsed in our inner
room (leaving Ben and me
to the army bunks in the other)
I see your grin unsharpening
those sharp eyes (your daughters have
your eyes)   I see you on the roof
of the LBR* on a warm
April Sunday helping me

cram for our Psych exam
oranges and peanuts-in-the-shell
along with all that jargon
(we pitched the shells off the edge
kept what we needed for chewing over)
I see you on the Lincoln Road
near midnight strip and run and
caper past St. Margaret's
goatish for our eyes Fredericton's

first streaker agnostic but given
to belting out hymns in every
church in town dragging us
along (just as in Baltimore
ten years later newly
ordained you dragged me from church
to church opening cupboards and modelling
vestments richer than the window-saints')

*Lady Beaverbrook Residence

Monica says you took her on a
whirlwind tour of England's
cathedrals just last October
flagging only at Lincoln   We should
have seen it coming in your passion
for truth and aesthetics in your long
surgeon's fingers unsqueamish
concocting Spanish rice for our guests or
cleaning up the mess of worms
your cat Therese deposited

by our table   You even labelled
a painting turned messy *Bandage
from a Festered Wound*   And you gave
yourself to the bandaging of wounds
you and Esperanza in NYC
Esperanza whose name means
hope title of your first poem
written all those years before
you saw her   *Hope* with its *sea*

of silver radiance   Esperanza
yesterday radiant and ready
impresario to your grand requiem
where Dumitru's violin and Lucina's
viola rhymed Pleyel's autumnal
Andante and so re-issued your poem
and its *lyric scarlet streak / among
the harmonies of softer yellow strings*
just as you'd have wanted

BEAR STORIES

For Don's 72nd

I

Magi was it? Or shepherds who first
saw shapes bigger than dippers
in the night sky   Maybe it was
camel drivers loaded with silk
and nutmeg along the Silk Road
to Samarkand or some such oasis

Do you see what I see?
No   What?   It's a bear
a big one   See his nose
points to that star the rest
all turn on   Can't you see it?
Yes   and a little one too
See   his nose is that very star
the other's pointing to

Two of them they saw as kids
do just by joining the dots
Some other night-watcher
must have added a Hunter and two
Dogs that chase Bear Little
and Bear Big around the Pole
without ever getting closer
season in and season out

Dad showed us how to find
the dippers   From them it was
an easy stretch to bears and hunters

2

Now bears are everywhere
in the Bible even ready
to devour brats who run after
prophets and call them names

We've seen them bumble
across the road on Route 7
or 8 and in their brick dungeon
at Rockwood Park poor moulting
bears behind bars fouled
in their own dung

The smell of it
hung on and gave us a name
for Bearstink Mountain a raspberry
rich hill we found once
near the cottage we rented
on Belleisle Bay

We didn't stay to pick
but left that summer ripeness
to the one with squatter's rights

3

When Mum was putting her to bed
in our dining-room after
her shock and total sleeplessness
Grandma saw bears   *You wouldn't sleep*
in that room for all the money
in the world now   would you?
Why not   Ma? Why ever not?
There's bears in that room
There's bears I tell you

92

4

Thanksgiving weekend Don
you reported a bear on the trail
the Nashwaak we'd just walked
from the old railroad bridge to our
place a bear asleep you saw
when you took a detour to your
favourite stopping place behind
a clump of trees a bear so sound
asleep you weren't afraid   It lay
half on its belly half on its side
its snout couched groundward

Maybe it's a dead bear
or a dog Didn't you check? No
but I'm sure it's alive It was so
slack and relaxed kind of blissful
in its sleep not stiff at all

That's how you described it
and you didn't want to disturb it
in case it was having a dress rehearsal
for a much longer sleep

93

5

So we have our own backyard
bear story to go along with
Grandma's and Grandpa's   The night
for instance when the men were all
in the woods and Grandpa's sisters
the timid ones were visiting put to bed
in the downstairs spare room
In the night they rousted up Grandma
Ruth Ruth there's a bear outside
It's clawing to get in and we're
scared half to death   Grandma pooh-poohed
their fears but couldn't silence them

So she grabbed the axe
fresh in from the grindstone
and in her nightgown charged
out of doors and loped around
the house chopping the ground
in front of her and hollering
If there's anything out here
now you git!

And Grandma quelled the bears
in our house too. She used to laugh
with us at them before she went
back up home for the last time
where hers really were waiting
in the orchard where she fell

6

Don I saw your bear still
there asleep just as you described
quiet as a furry dusky rock
half-hidden in tall grass but
unmistakably ursine unmistakably

A ONE-SIDED CALL TO A
MANY-SIDED MAN

You magnificent red-bearded
runt runt?   Hardly   You see
what happens when I try
to address you as you did
John Keats   Junkets you dubbed him

Now I'm almost afraid to call you
scared you'll drop by grab me
by the shoulder shake me and say
What's this foolishness
you're up to?

You were never simply
a simple man and no box
I might contrive can
contain you any more than
your little poem could box
John Keats runt though he was

Alden how many times have I
called you these eighteen years?
Whenever I put my eyes to a page
of yours you come up true
your voice the grit and honey of it
and your syllables pushed out clean
but not without effort after
your radical duel with cancer

And your chuckles they come too
never belly laughs but just as catching
I can see you now your head
thrust back beard heavenward
your merriment a praise for the gift of it

I read you in silence the better
to hear   You slow down and speed up
to measure out your measures and make them
sing   And you make your tones
up and down the scale not as an actor might
theatrical but as soul of the stuff
you hold in your head

No-one listening would doubt
for a second your poem's truth
or your truth's poetry though hardly
less at home than at their own
kitchen table just at talk with you

I can hear you in debate
that last night with Johnny
serious engaged but not solemn
You gave as good as you got
full weight but with a lightness
that belied weightiness   Johnsonian?
Yes but in a way the great man
whom you loved might not have
countenanced   Still I doubt
his bearhugs at the midnight hour
were as bearish as yours when you
held us back from going home
to bed too soon

Alden you weren't ever simply
a simple man   Lord help me
not ever to forget it

Saltiness and razor-edged wit
gentleness when gentleness
was called for   But what about
your anger? Wrath not always
righteous   I might have done
without that if it didn't mean
doing without you   Rage
against what or whom could you
really say? Furies you grappled with
turned fantasies to plays of light
on blackness poems that shine
in on my own dark nights things
I recognize but seldom reckon with

You made free to make myths
the more far-fetched the better
with yourself your demons and even
with us to make us feel larger
than ourselves or smaller
if we insisted on pinching
high spirits into low letters

Deception you knew well
is most often self-deception and
poetry most often an antidote
to that as Elizabeth said
a small day of judgment
sinners that we are

98

Your folly unfooled was play
a child's for the delight
of children   It helped to keep
your eyes clear and ascant
the world in kinship
with the Son of Man's

Now what about pictures?
the visible you   I can call up
one on the ferry wharf
at Borden PEI after a round
of readings you pale and queasy
after too much bedtime talk
and bedtime gin and maybe
too much of that other reader
not me oh never me
that man as tall as you but thin
thirty years your senior poet
and a good one westerner
in fringed buckskin he capered
like a goat and talked down
to the students in their lingo
digging this and digging that

99

I can hear during his reading
in the Charlottetown SUB
a hoarse whisper in my ear
He's boring the ass off
these kids Bob   And at St.John's
a night or two before from your bed
you nightcap at hand   *What a sad*
old man a sad sad old man
Will you promise me something Bob?
If I ever get like that will you
just take me out and shoot me?
words that twisted out of you boozy
a mix of pity and contempt
fear and compassion but fun too
as they often were

What happened to the picture?
Forgive me my dotage my
anecdotage   I've left you standing
wobbly on the wharf cigarette in hand
eyes squinted shut or almost shut
and me with two tourists Americans likely
excited to see a boy fishing
off the pier drag up a sculpin
and lay it on the wharf to wriggle out
its death throes ugliest mugged
of all God's fishes which we
gaped and tittered at while you

stood aloof your eyes if anywhere
out in the Strait   Only after you'd gone
did I find among your things
unpublished and maybe for you
unfinished that strong poem
"The Sculpin" that showed just how aware
a poet's half-awareness can be

Well Alden isn't it time to say
good-night? to let you
let me go?   I like to think of us
both of us as waiting to be held
in arms bigger than our own
So I'll sign off as you would
Keep the faith old friend keep the faith

For the opening of the Alden Nowlan Festival
at Old Government House in Fredericton
on 25 October, 2001

102

Hitherto ROBERT GIBBS has been known to Oberon readers as a writer of fiction. *I've Always Been Sorry for Decimals*, *A Mouth-Organ for Angels* and *Angels Watch Do Keep* all appeared under the Oberon imprint. Robert Gibbs has retired from teaching and lives in Fredericton, NB.